BY GREEN FIG

How the UNIVERSE started?!

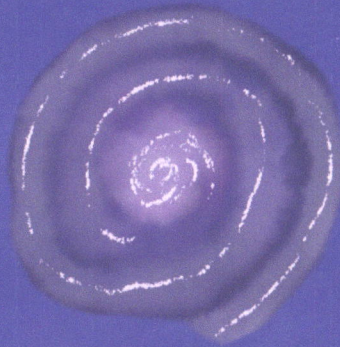

DESIGN & ART BY

Guzel Murtazina

Green Fig

Proud Muslim Kids

NAME _____

NOTE:

Pictures in this book
don't correspond to reality

Publisher: Green Fig
Pennsylvania. USA
gogreenfig.com

DEAR PARENTS & EDUCATORS

The story of the creation of the universe is of utmost importance for our children. In today's world, they are exposed to various theories on this subject. It is crucial to protect our children, whether they are young, pre-teens, or teens, by acquainting them with the truth about the origin of this whole universe that it was created by Allāh, the One who brought everything into existence. Allāh willed the occurrence of this universe, that's why it came to be. God brought it from non-existence to existence.

It is essential to understand that the universe did not exist eternally with Allāh. Only Allāh existed in eternity, as mentioned in religious texts. In Surat al-Ḥadid, verse #3, God said:

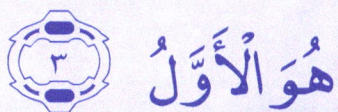

$$هُوَالْأَوَّلُ ﴿٣﴾$$

which means "God is the only One without a beginning."

The Prophet, may peace be upon him, further affirmed this by stating:

$$"كان الله ولم يَكُنْ شَيْءٌ غَيْرُهُ"$$

meaning "God existed eternally, and nothing else existed" (Narrated by al-Bukhariyy).

3

This book serves as a clear presentation of the facts about the beginning of the universe, as mentioned in the Qur'an and the prophetic sayings that explicitly declare God as the creator of this entire universe. The religious texts are too abundant to mention them in this note. Here are few examples:

Allāh said:

الْحَمْدُ لِلَّهِ الَّذِي خَلَقَ السَّمَوَاتِ وَالْأَرْضَ وَجَعَلَ الظُّلُمَاتِ وَالنُّورَ ﴿١﴾

[Al-An'ām: 1], which means "Praise be to Allāh, who created the heavens and the earth and created the darkness and the light."

Allāh also said:

﴿٧﴾ خَلَقَ السَّمَوَاتِ وَالْأَرْضَ فِي سِتَّةِ أَيَّامٍ وَكَانَ عَرْشُهُ عَلَى الْمَاءِ

[Hūd: 7], which means "He created the heavens and the earth in six days and His Throne was above the water."

Moreover, Allāh said:

﴿٣٠﴾ وَجَعَلْنَا مِنَ الْمَاءِ كُلَّ شَيْءٍ حَيٍّ

[Al-Anbiyā': 30], which means "And We made from water every living thing (and non-living things)."

How the Universe Started? also introduces, in a simplified manner suitable for children, the logical proof concerning the necessity of a Creator. The universe did not create itself; this concept is mentally impossible since it implies the existence of the universe before it actually existed. A matter did not create the universe, as any matter lacks willpower and requires a creator itself. Furthermore, the universe did not come into existence as a result of the so-called "Big Bang theory" or any other falsehoods.

We sincerely hope that this book proves to be highly beneficial. We value your feedback and invite you to reach out to us at info@gogreenfig.com.

Warm regards,
Green Fig Team

In Eternity, only God existed. Nothing else existed.

Eternity

No
darkness

No
light

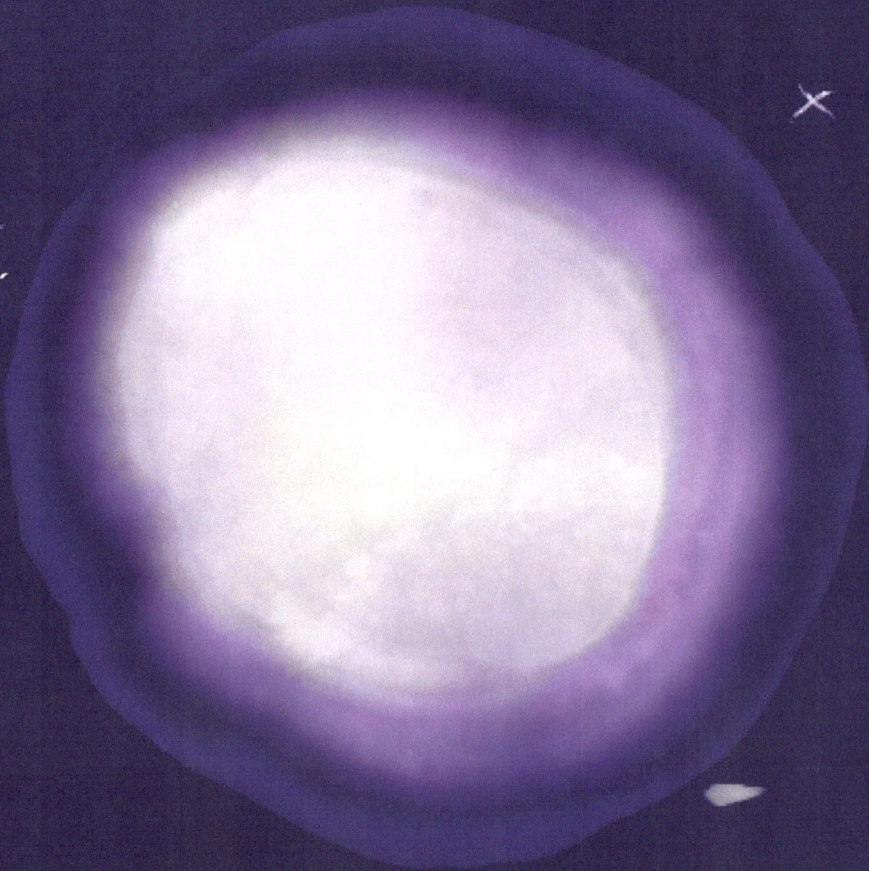

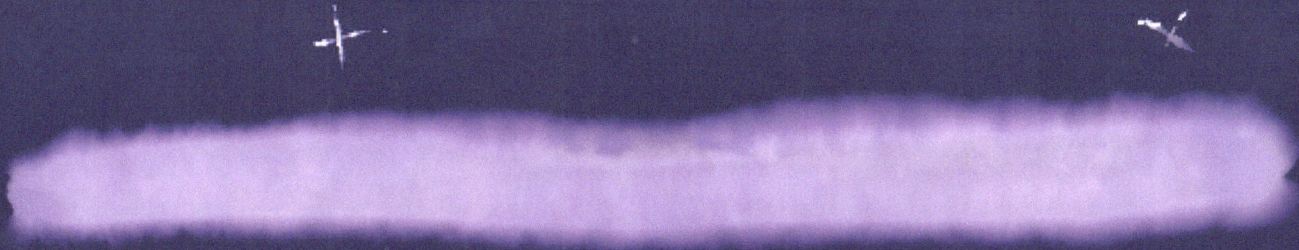

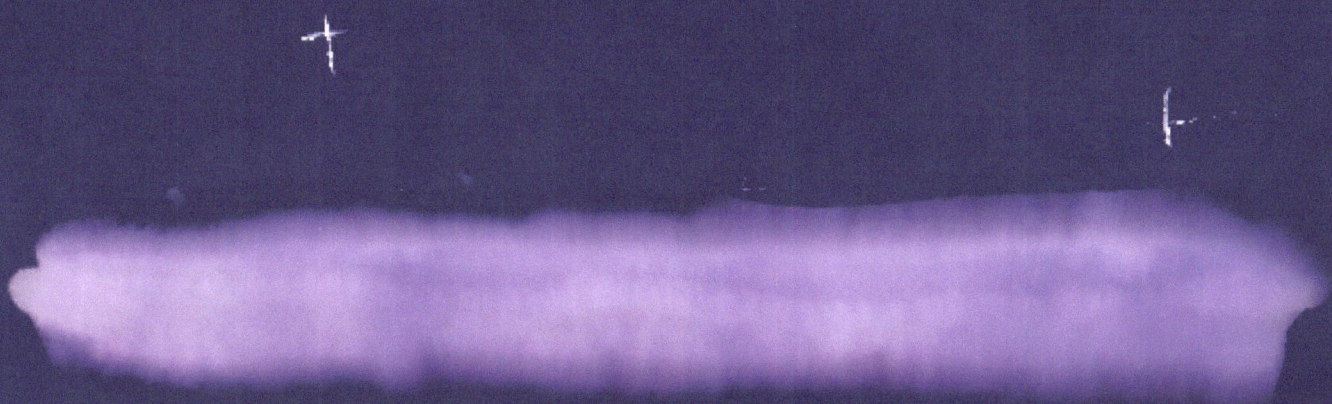

**No
space**

9

No
heavens

No
earth

No
humans

No
animals

No
place

up

↑

left ←   → right

↓

down

14

and No
time

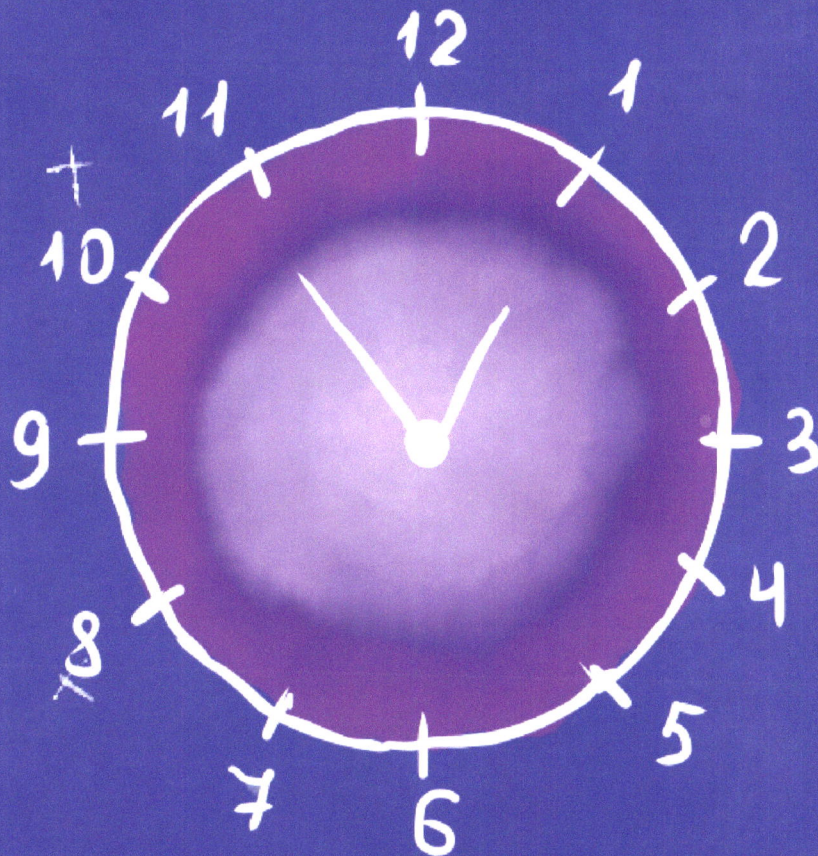

This means God does not have a beginning; God always existed.

Everything other than
God,
has a beginning,

a start.

God created everything. He brought the whole universe from non-existence to existence.

non-existence

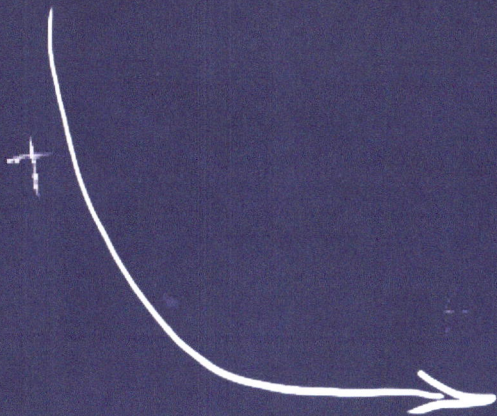

existence

19

The first thing that God
created was the
original water.

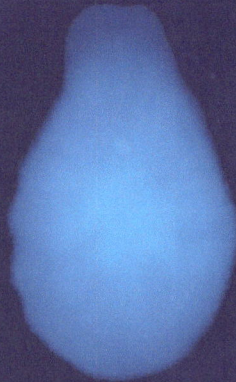

الماء

From this water God created everything else.

From water,
God created the Throne over this water. The throne is a very-very big structure, bigger than anything else God created.
It is a platform with pillars like a table has four legs.

العرش

The Throne

العَرْش

Then God created the Upper Pen. This pen is different than the pen we write with. It is as tall as the distance between earth and the first sky.

القلم الأعلى

The Upper pen

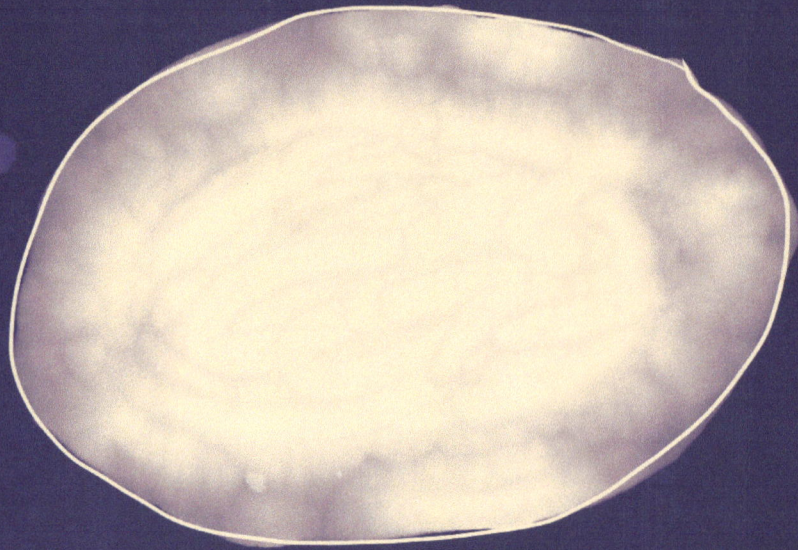

Then God created the Guarded Tablet, which is in the shape of one giant pearl surrounded on both sides with rubies.

Its width is the traveling distance of 500 years.

اللوح المحفوظ

Guarded Tablet

width = 500 years travelling

The Pen wrote on the Tablet, without anyone holding it, everything that is going to happen until the Day of Judgment.

29

After 50,000 years, the heavens and earth were created in six days.

Each day of these was as long as 1000 of our years.

On Sunday and Monday, God created the earth.

On Tuesday and
Wednesday,
God created the
seven heavens.

On Thursday and Friday God created the mountains, rivers, trees, valleys and the other landmarks of the earth that make it easy to live on.

Close to the beginning
of Friday, God created
all the Angels
from light.

During the day of Friday too, God created Satan who is a genie and the head of the devils from a pure flame of fire that does not produce any smoke.

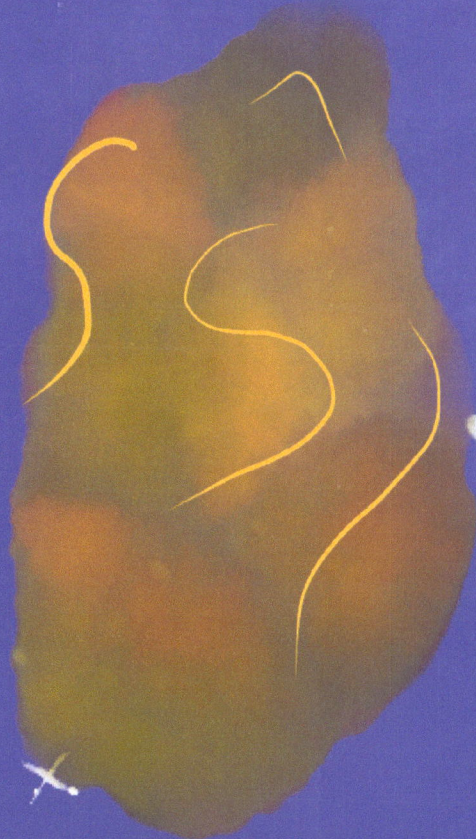

Toward the end of Friday, the first man, Adam, peace be upon him, was created. An angel was ordered to gather a handful from every type of soil on earth, the soft and the hard, the good and the bad, the red, the white, the black, the yellow and what in between.

The Angel took this soil to Paradise.

There, it was mixed with water from underneath The Throne. Soil and water became clay.

From this clay, the shape of Adam was formed.

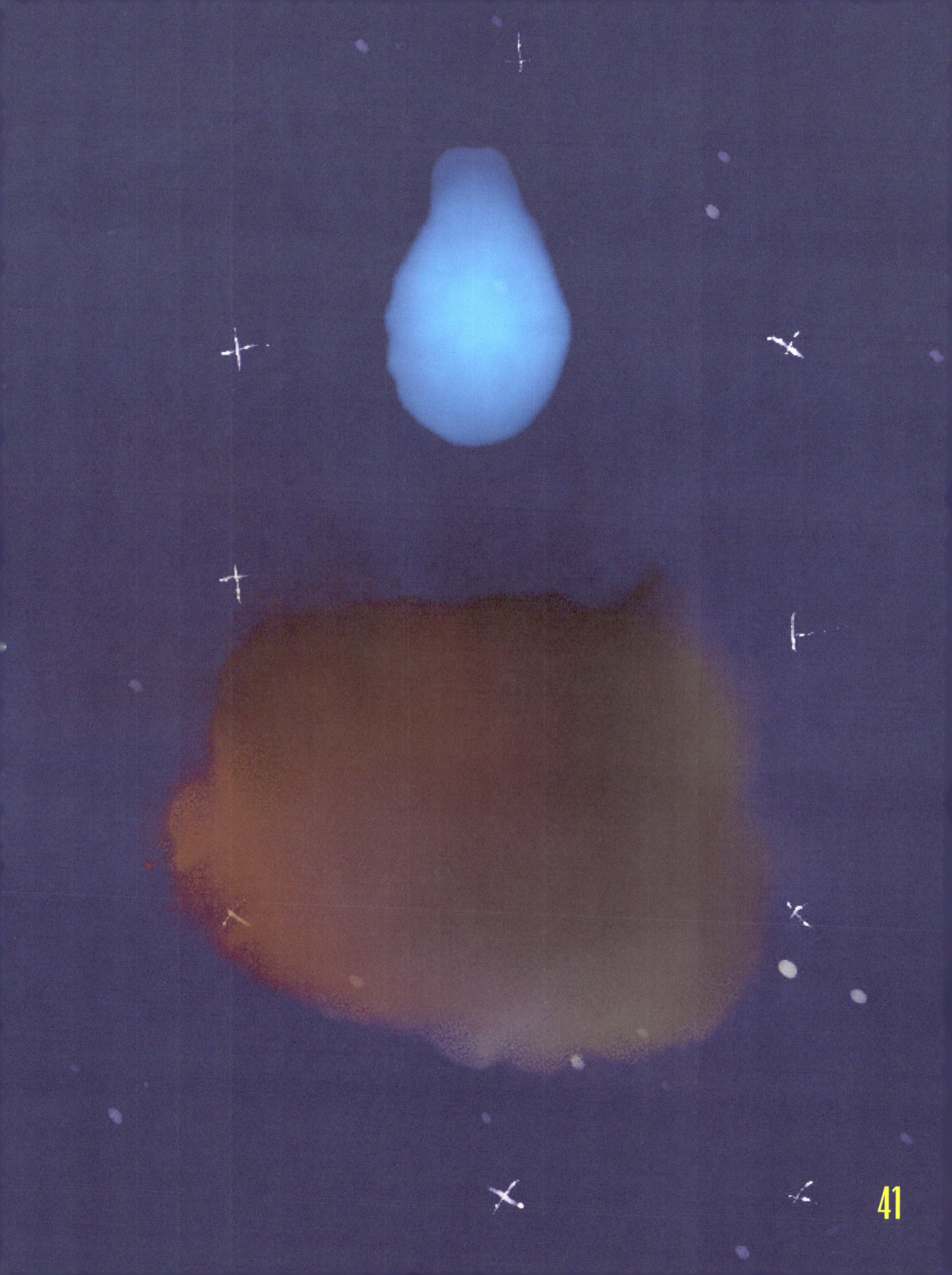

After the clay dried, God turned it into flesh, bones, and blood.

When the soul entered this body, Adam became alive.

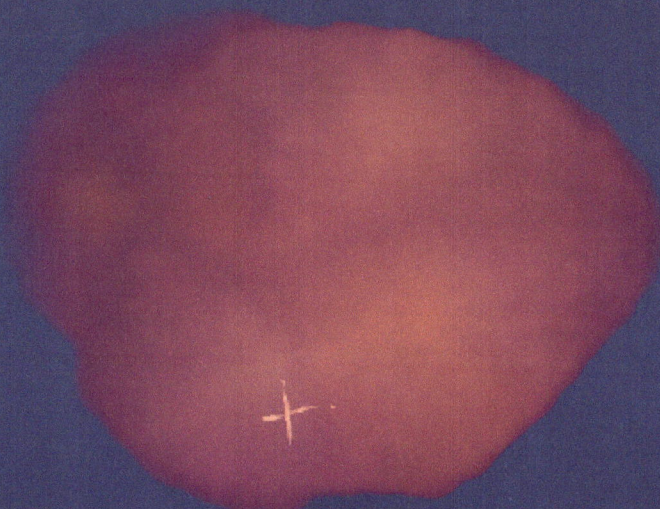

flesh

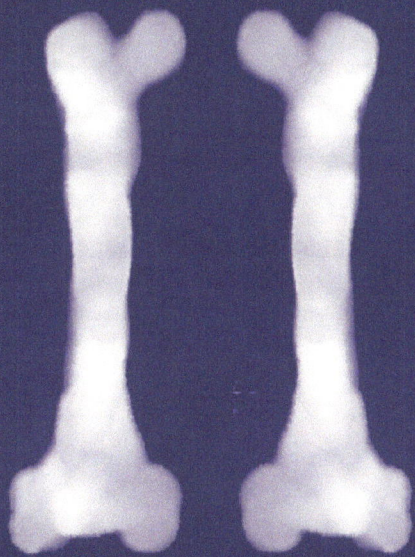

bones

blood

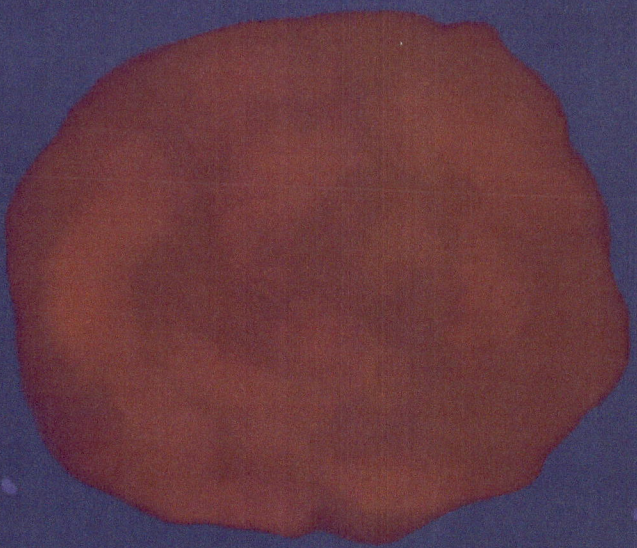

43

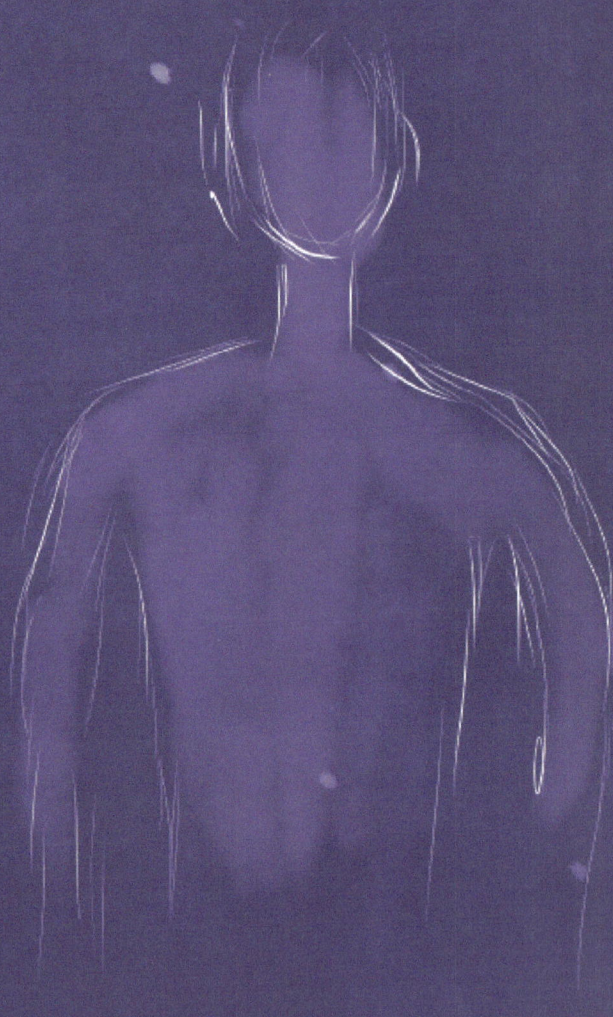

Adam was the last
kind of the creation:

humankind.

This is how the
universe started.

God created it!

The universe did not
happen without
a creator.
This cannot be.

A building needs a builder who built it.

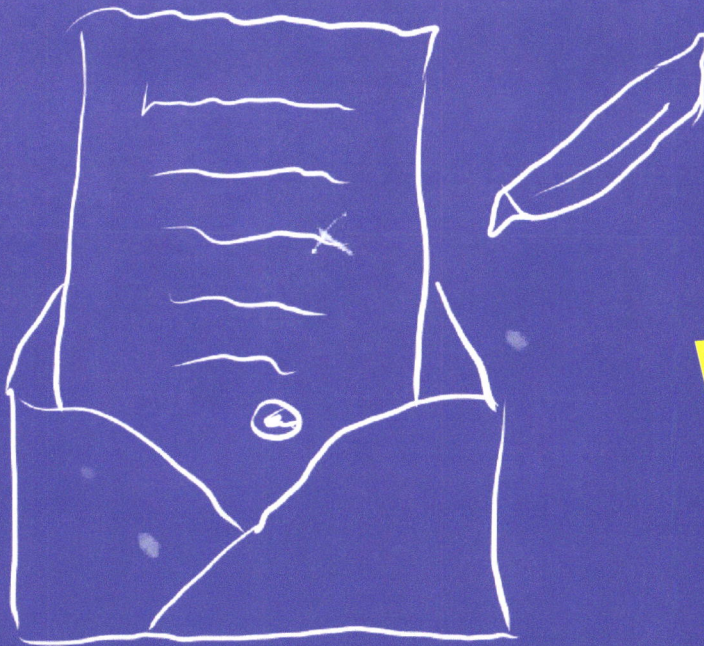

Something written needs a writer.

So how about this whole universe?!

Certainly, it needs a creator who is God, Allāh.

A matter with no will and no life did not create the universe.

All matters in the universe are created and need the Creator, God, who creates and changes them.

God is the Creator of this whole universe and everything that happens in it.

The Proud Muslim Kids series by Green Fig is a designed to engagingly teach youngsters basic concepts of Islam in a way that speaks to their hearts and minds. Each book in the series is crafted by a staff of qualified educators, writers, illustrators, parents and children. Not only is the Proud Muslim Kids series designed to supplement the early childhood and elementary Islamic curriculum, it is a great addition to any school or home library. Covering a wide variety of topics such as the Five Pillars of Islam, Islamic culture, and Islamic history, parents and children will return to these books and enjoy them together time and time again.

Publisher: Green Fig
Pennsylvania. USA
gogreenfig.com

www.ingramcontent.com/pod-product-compliance
Lightning Source LLC
LaVergne TN
LVHW072114070426
835510LV00002B/45